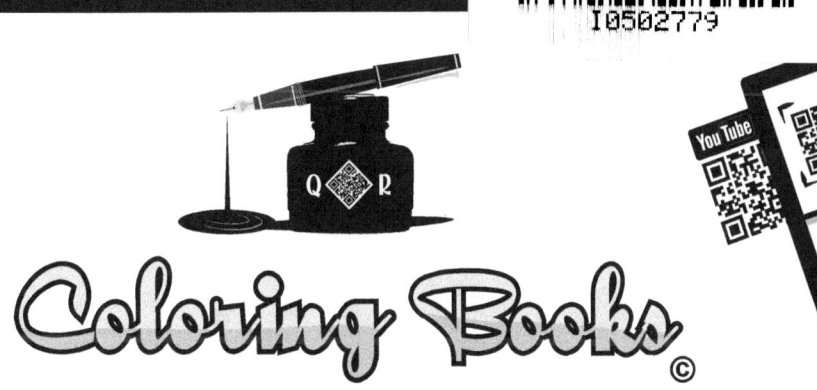

Coloring Books ©

Congratulations! You have chosen a unique coloring book that will provide entertainment, reduce stress and leave you with a feeling of tranquility.

- Download a free "QR Reader" to your cellphone

- Scan the code on each page

A video will pop up showing you the motivation for the drawing.

The idea is to relax and have fun. That combination requires that you set the scene for a great artistic experience. Betty Edwards book, "Drawing from the right side of the brain" is about a shift. Moving from verbal to a hard-to-access "R" -mode, a place where words aren't needed. Basically going to "The Zone".

The Zone is a cool place. In golf, it's called "unconscious confidence". No thought. To get there you have to know everything, then forget it.

First, clear your plate. Take out the trash, do your homework, pay bills, whatever. Eliminate your barriers for a more lengthy session. The idea is quality. If you can spend (5) good minutes coloring that's great, (30) minutes in the coloring zone…even better.

Crayon • Colored Pencils • Marker • Ball Point Pen • Lead Pencil • Chalk

Try different methods, combine them, let your mind explore. Lay out your tools so you can grab the easily. Turn on some good music, have your favorite drink in arm's reach.

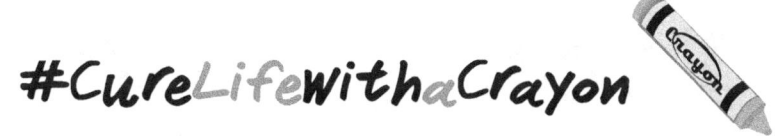

#CureLifewithaCrayon

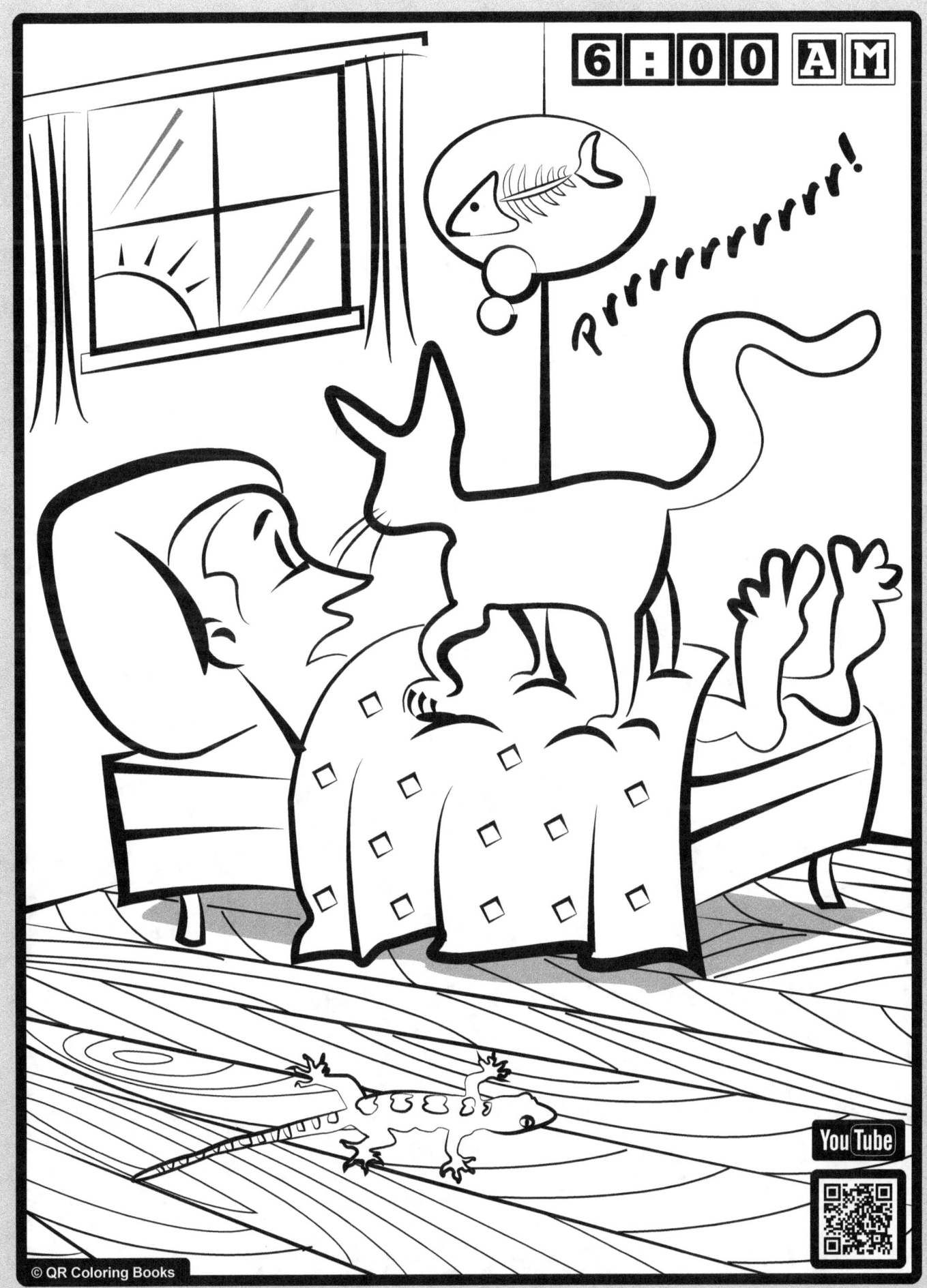

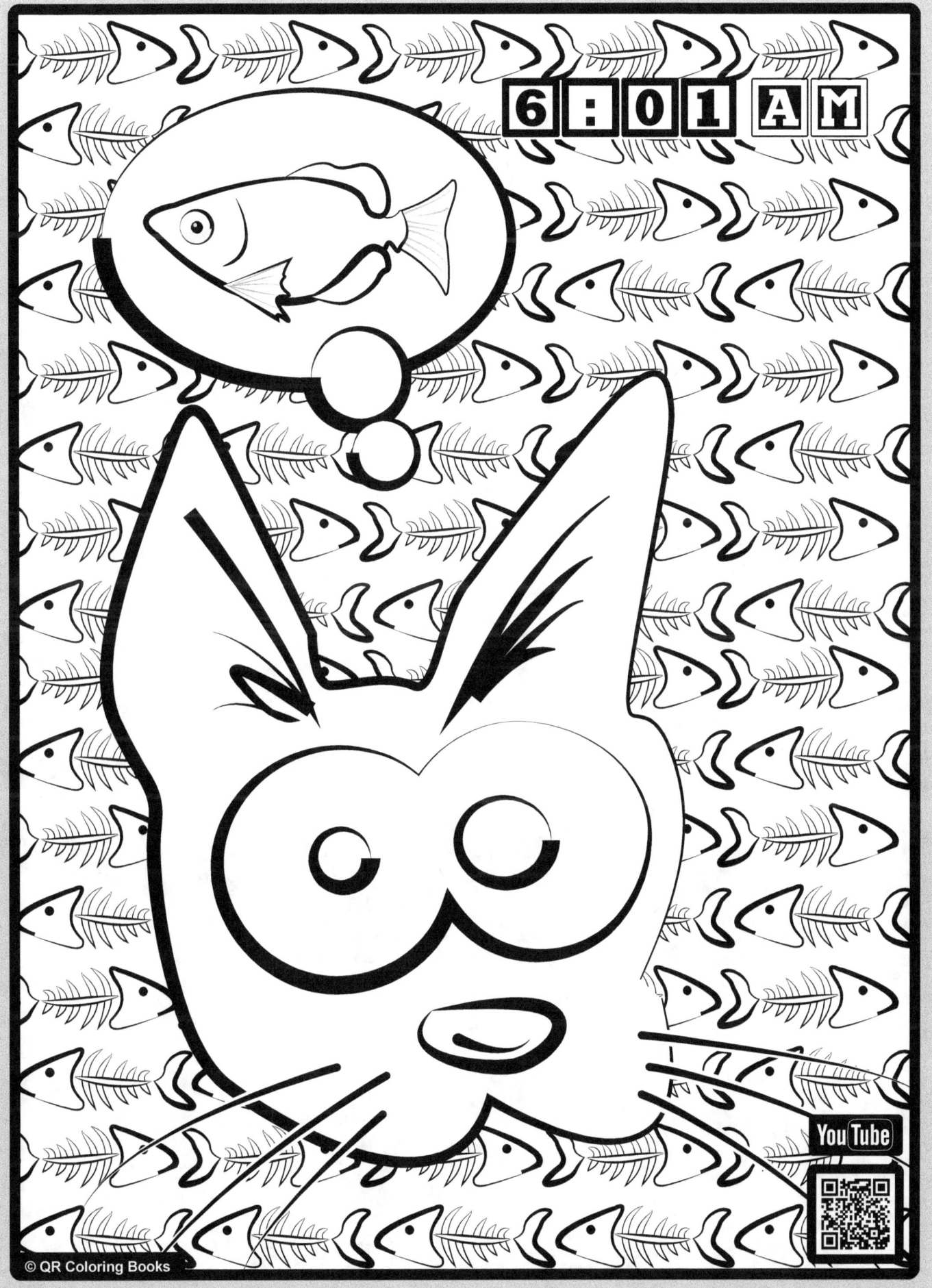

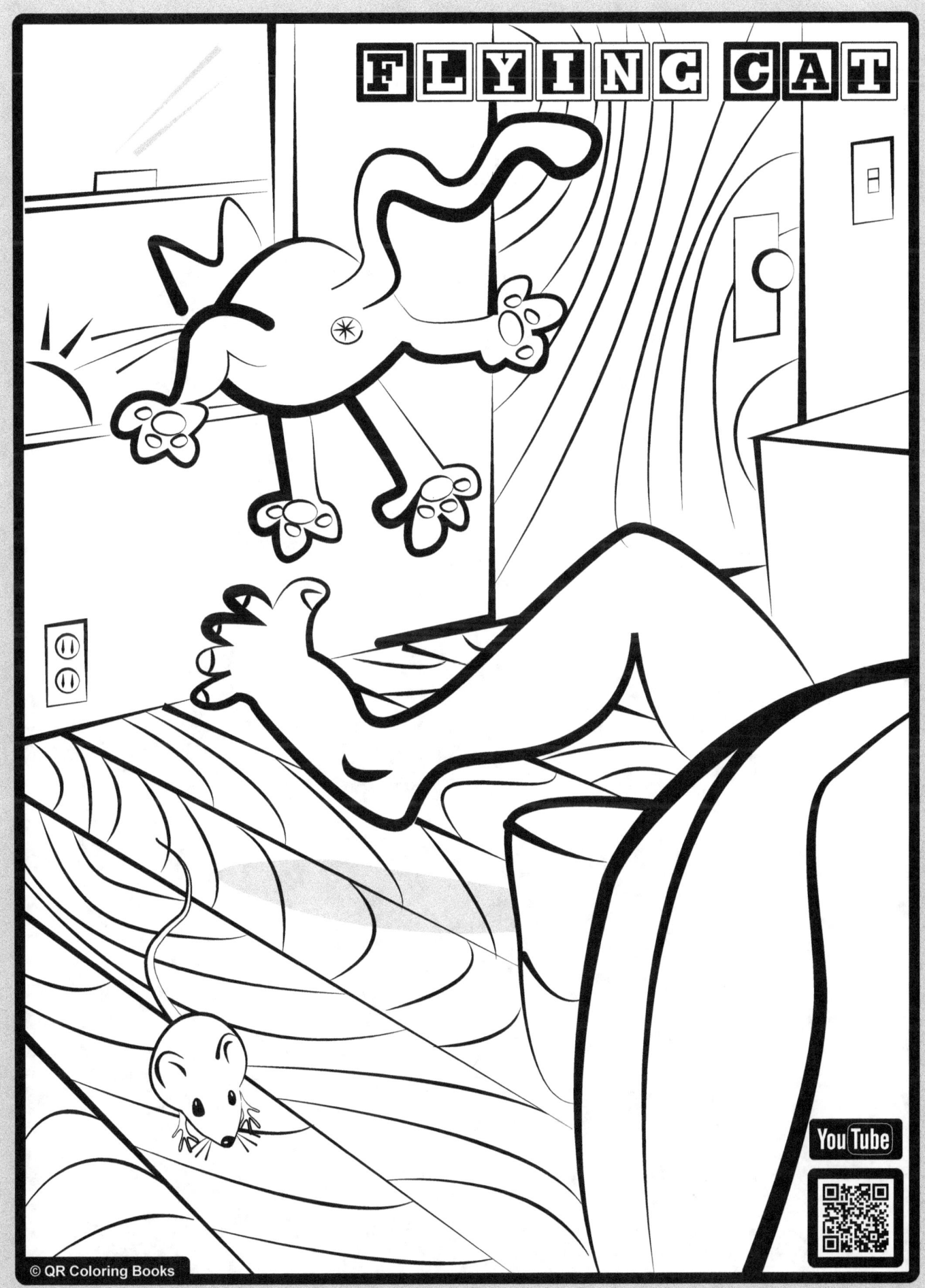

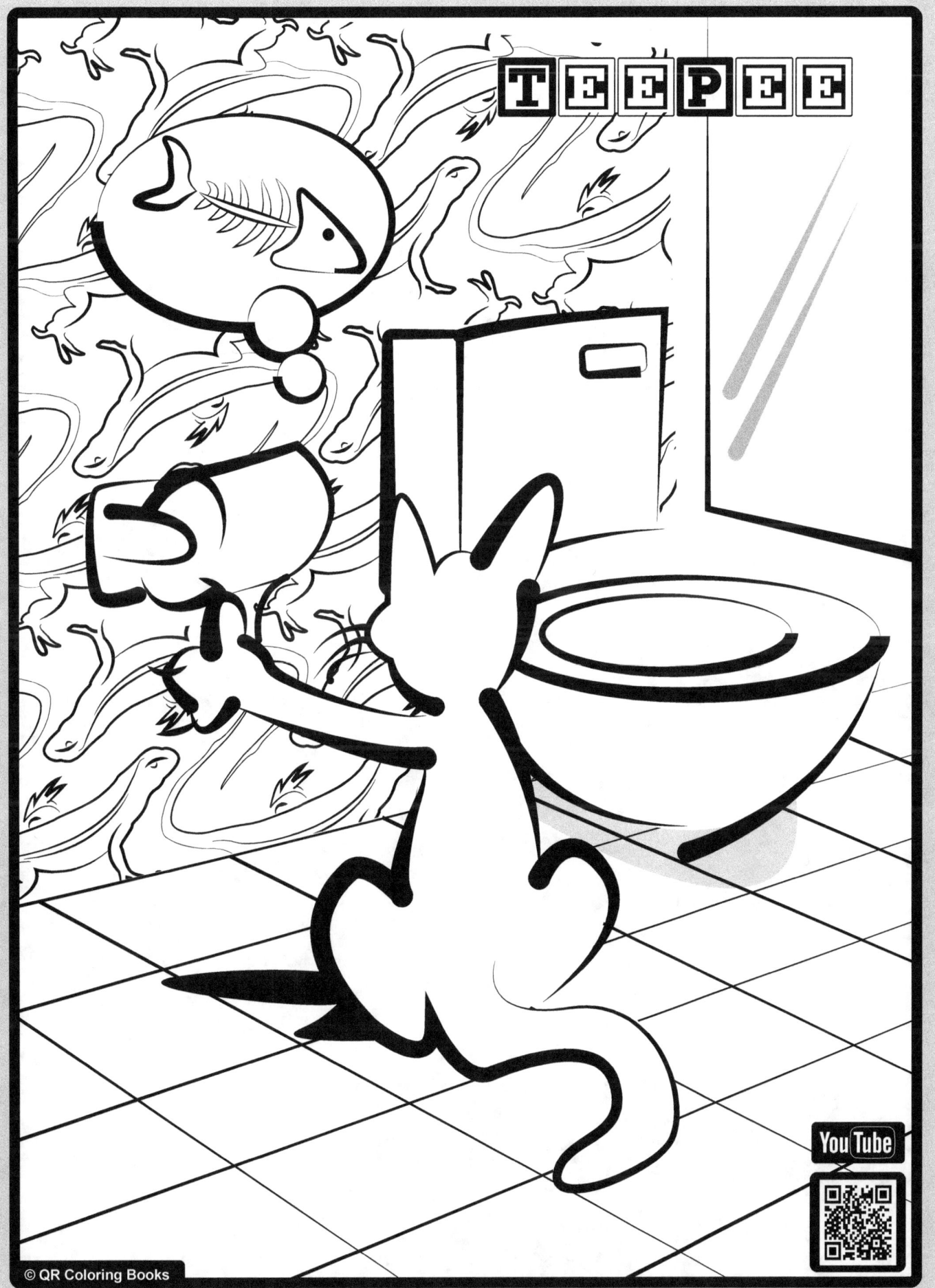

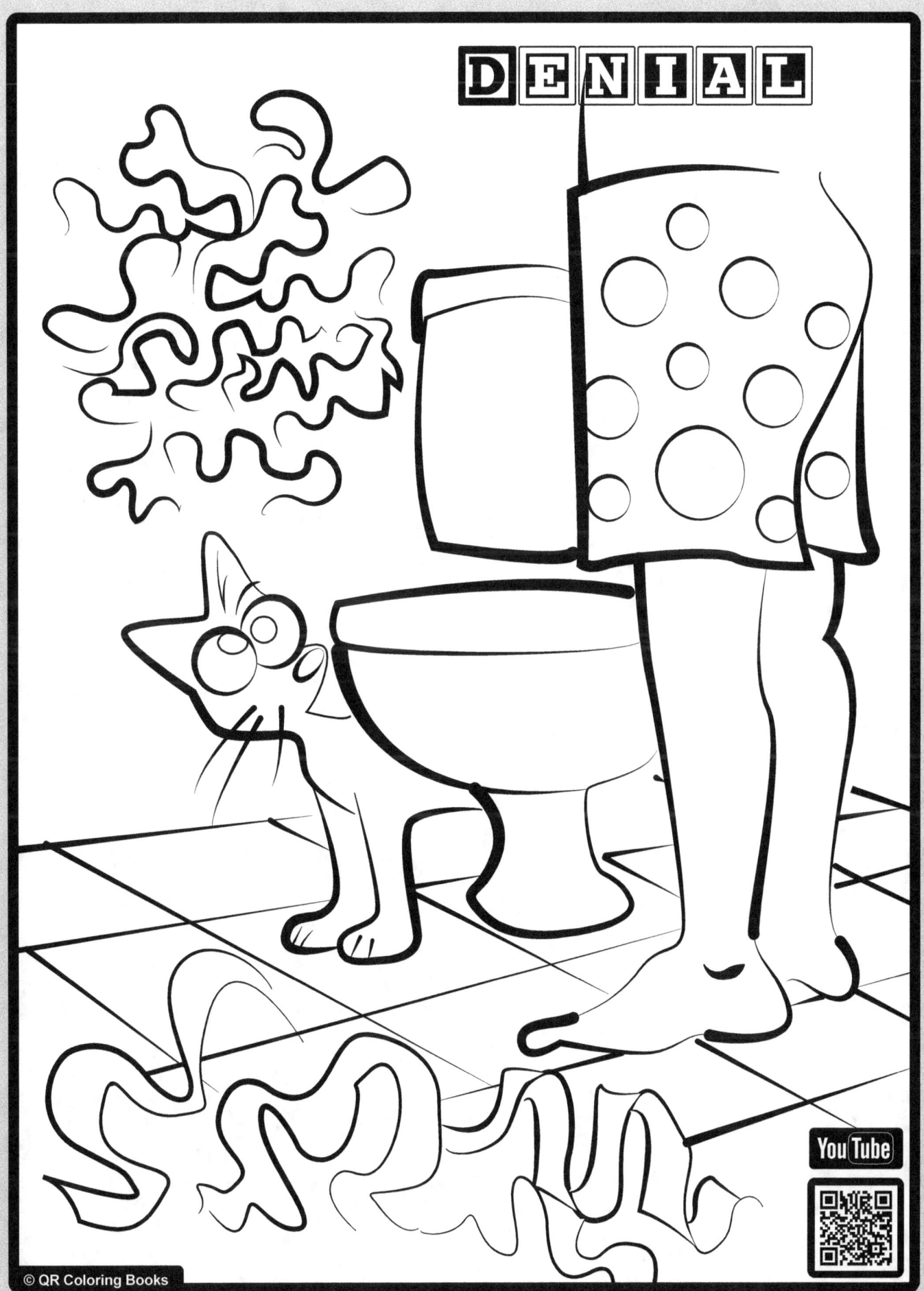

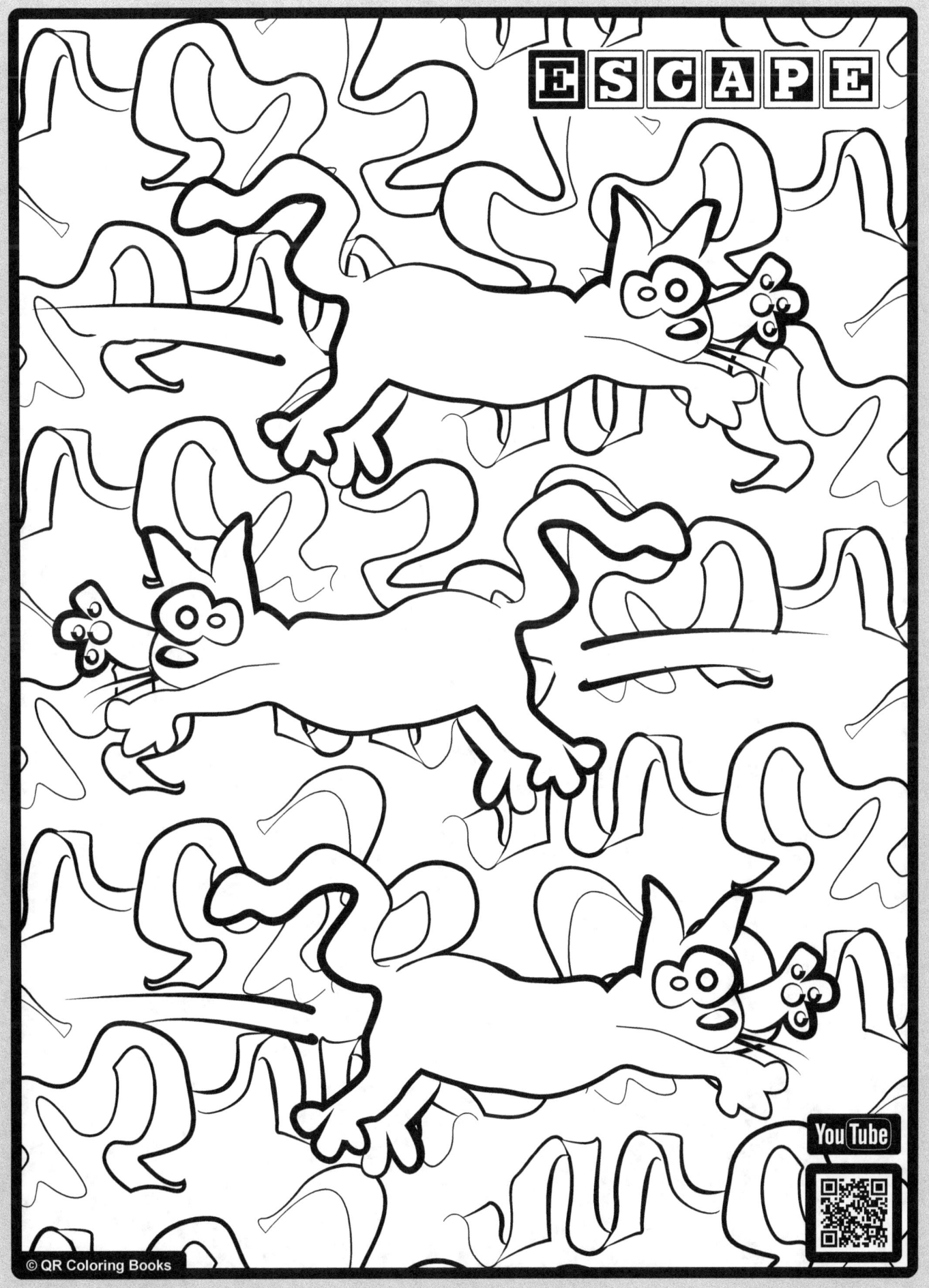

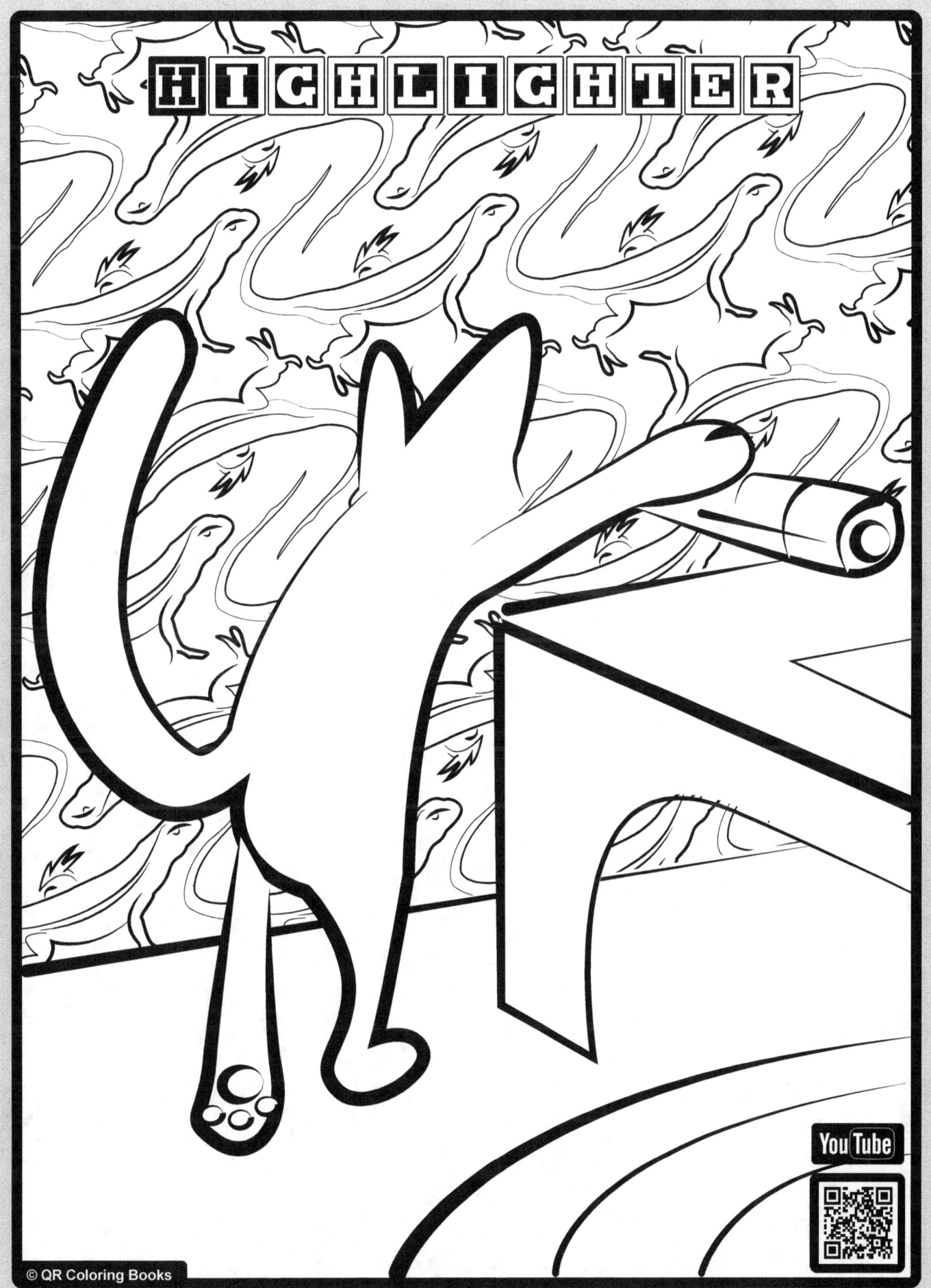

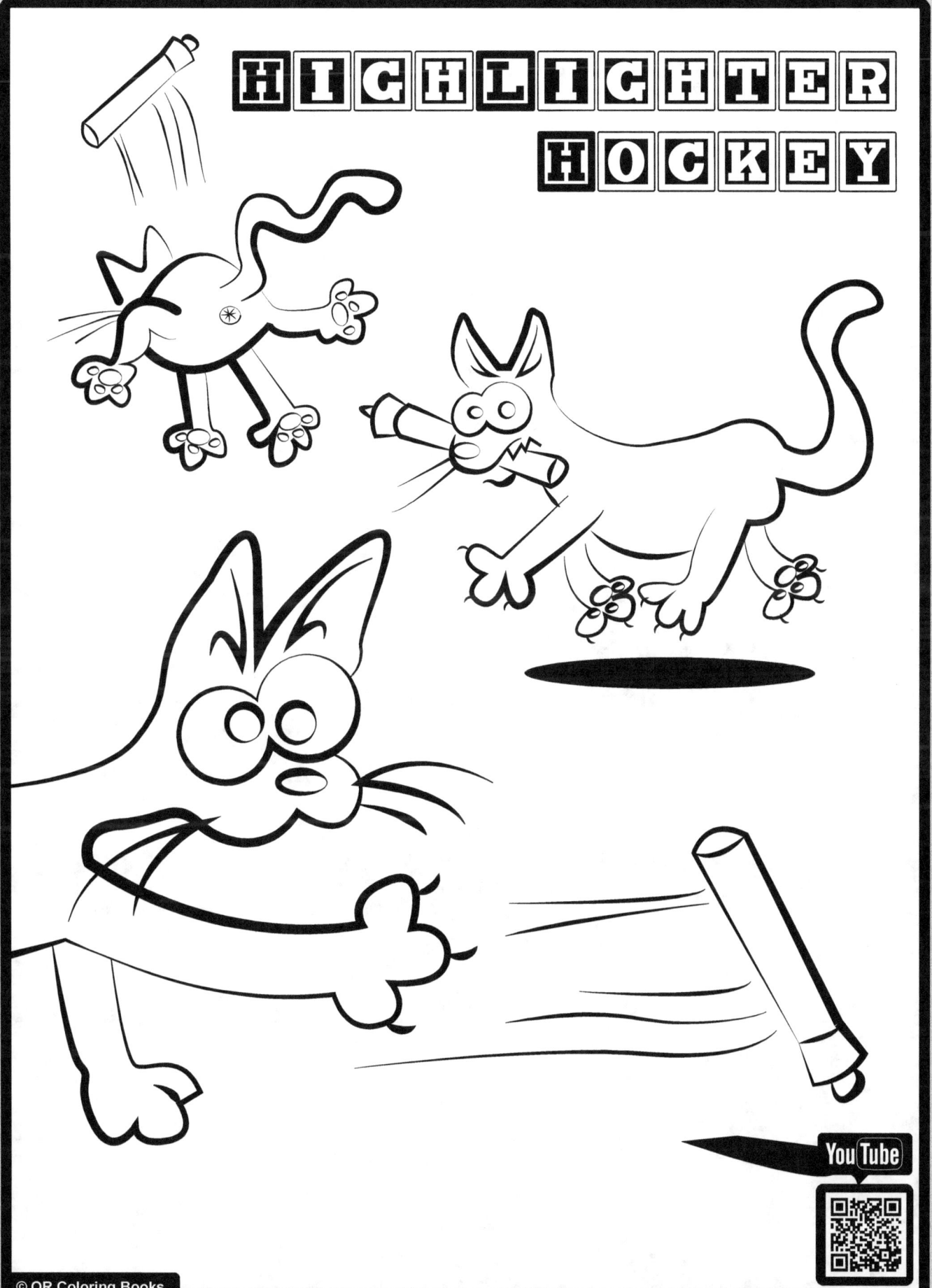

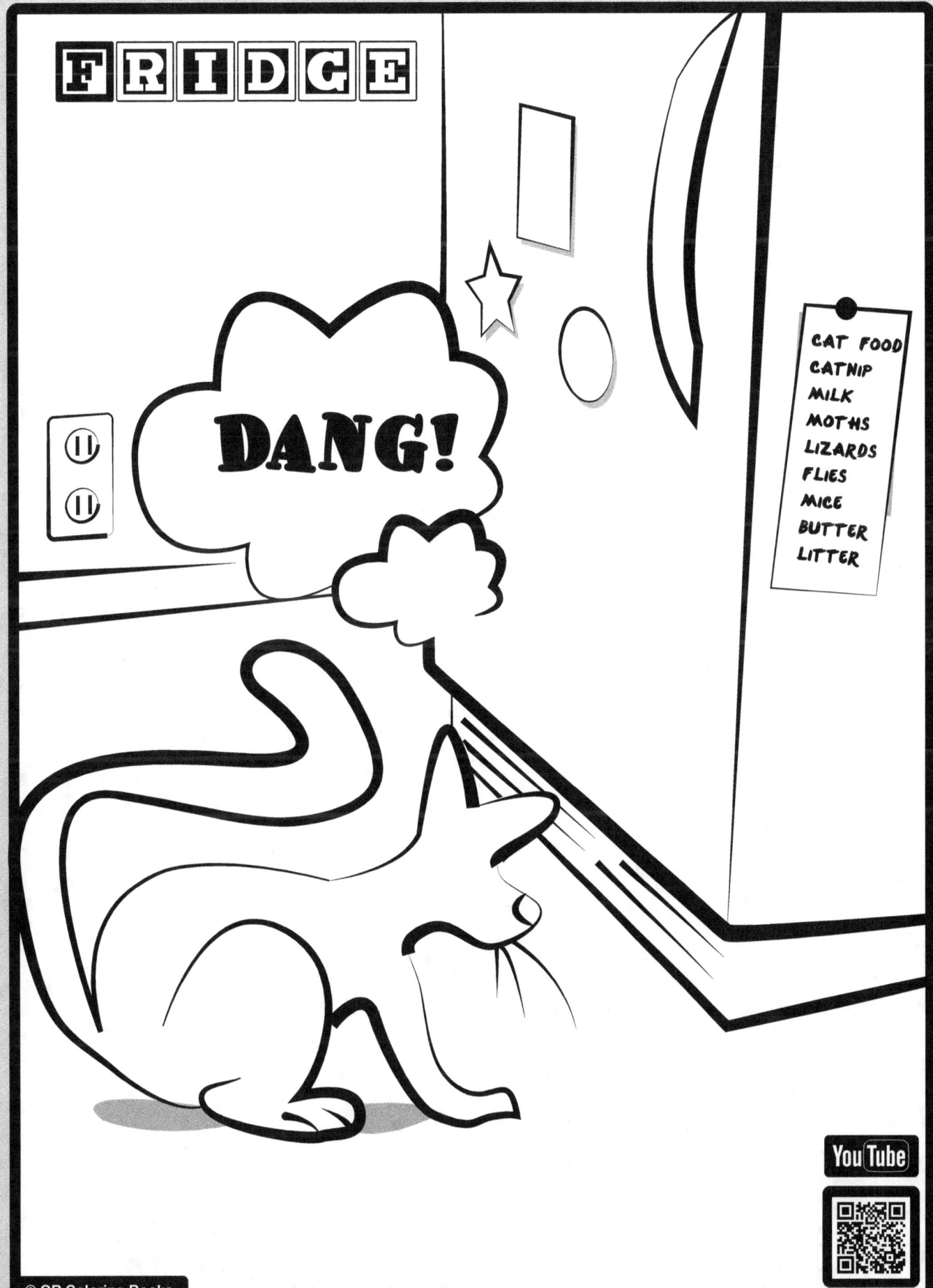

CLEAN

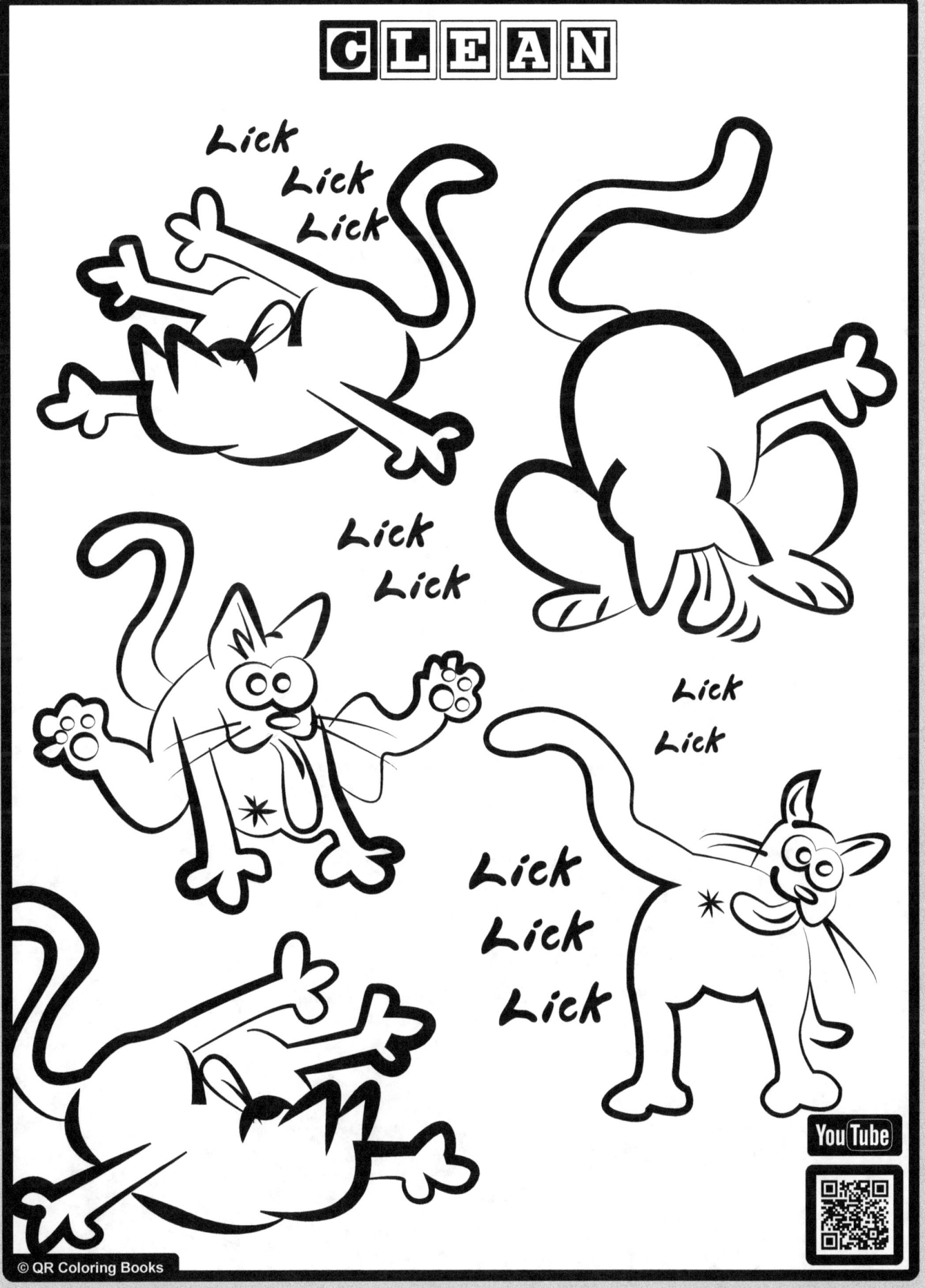

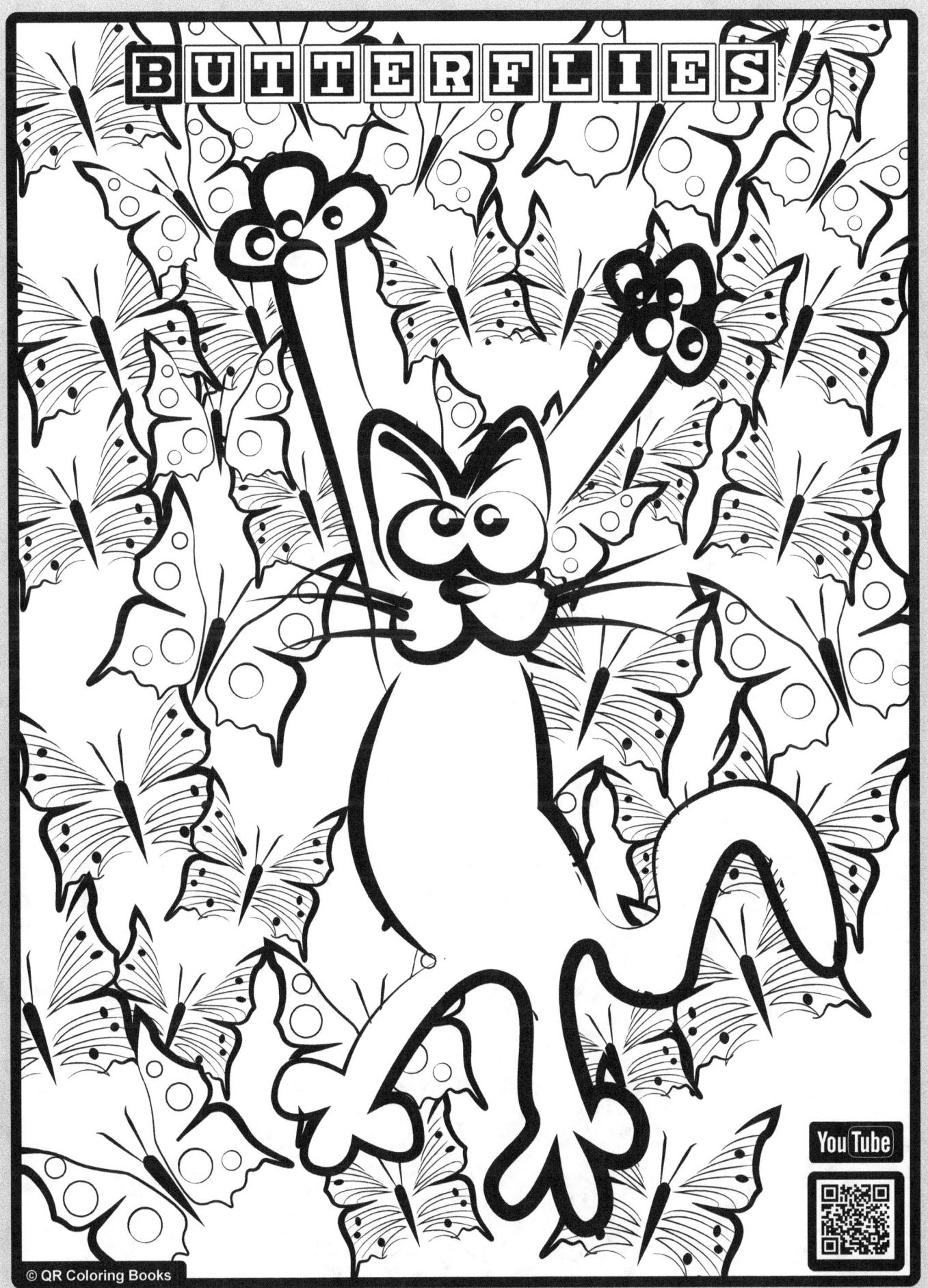

BUTTERFLIES

PLACES WHERE CATS FIT

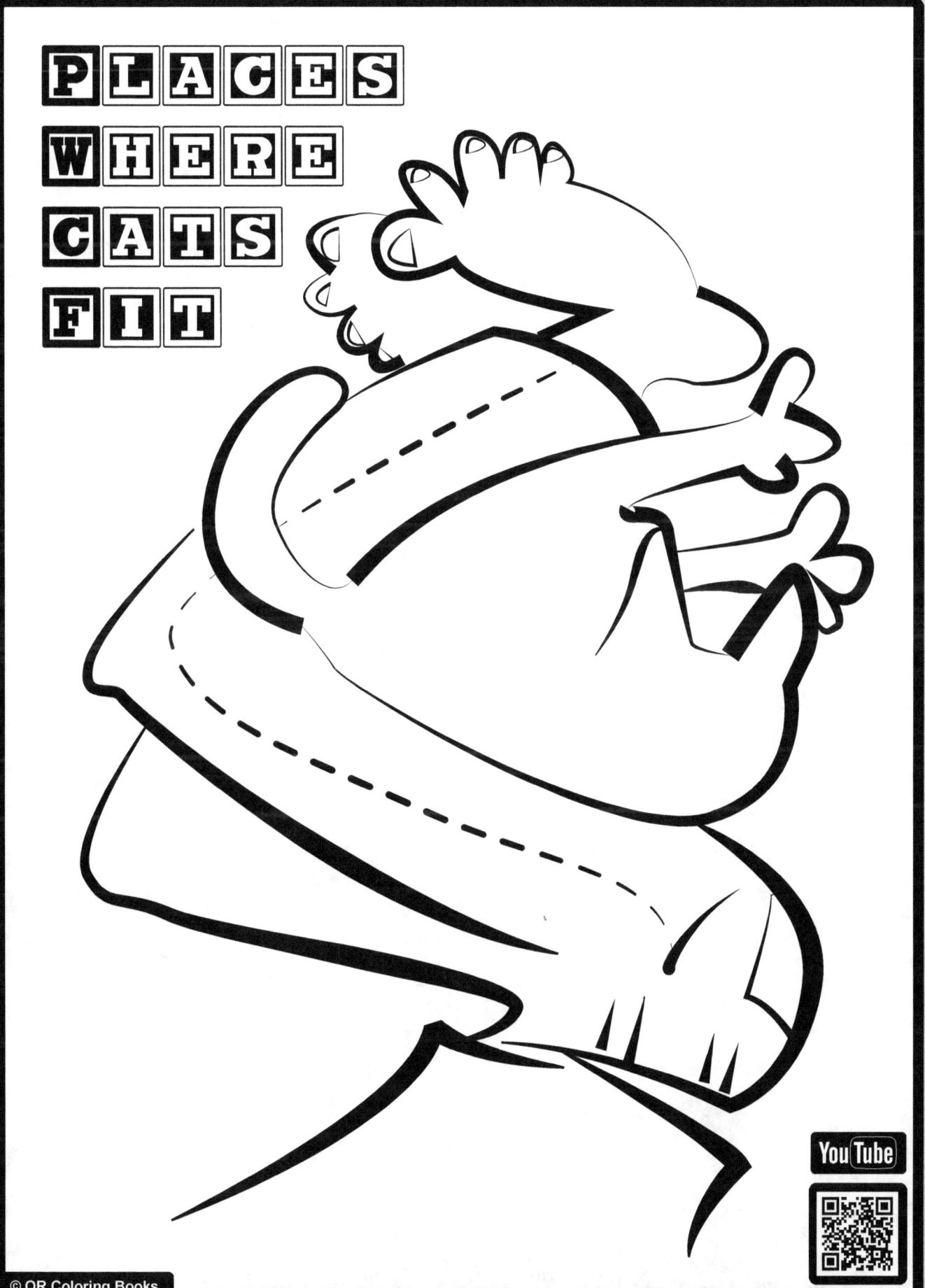

PET HEAD

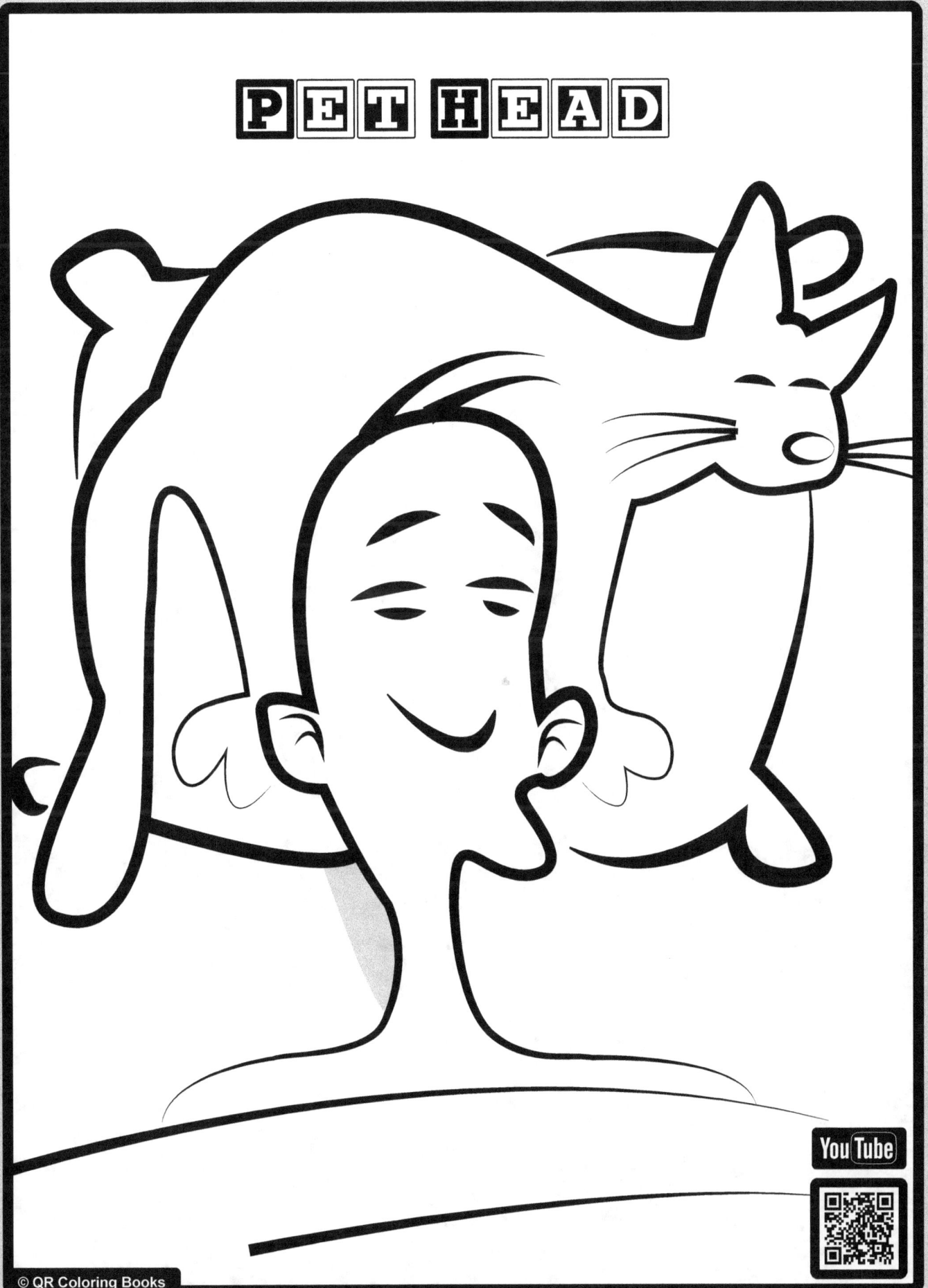

You Tube

CAT CHOW

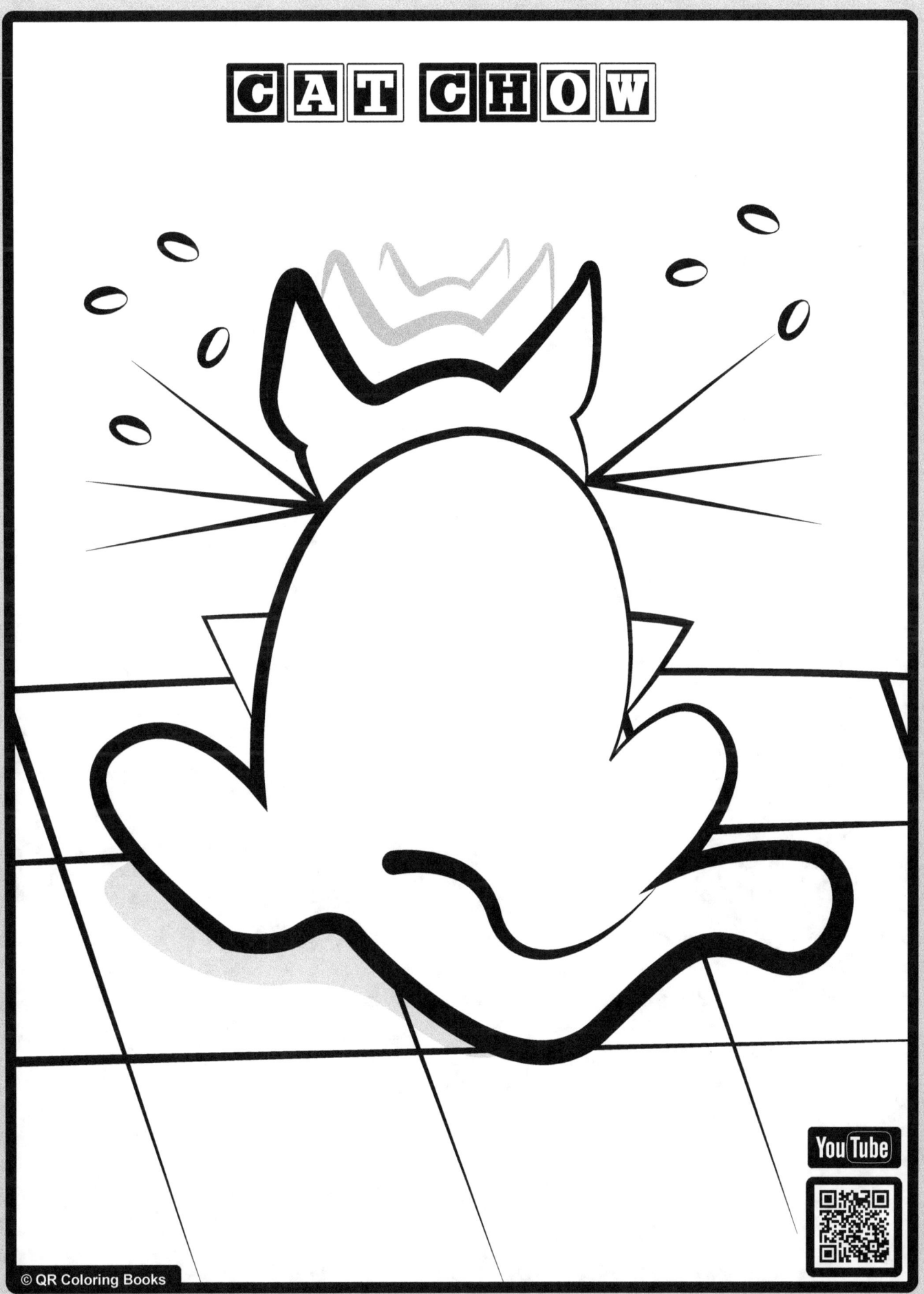

Cat Nap

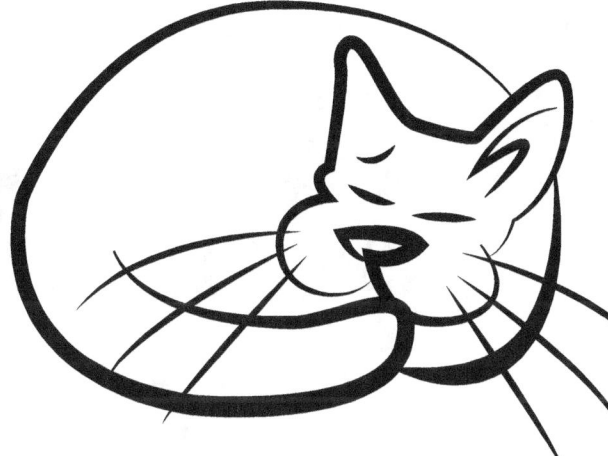

Cat Hip

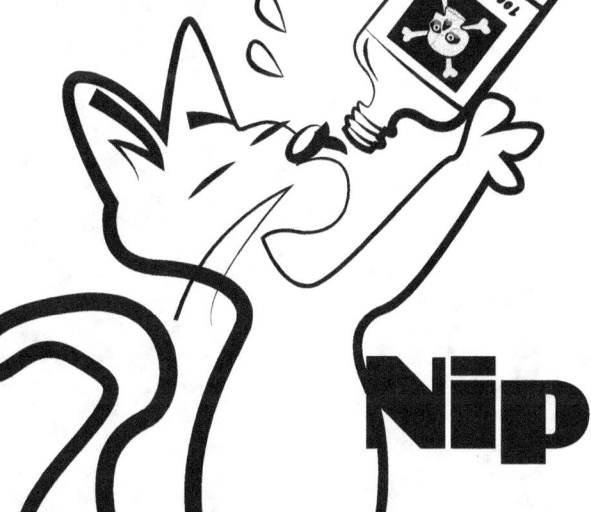

Cat Hat

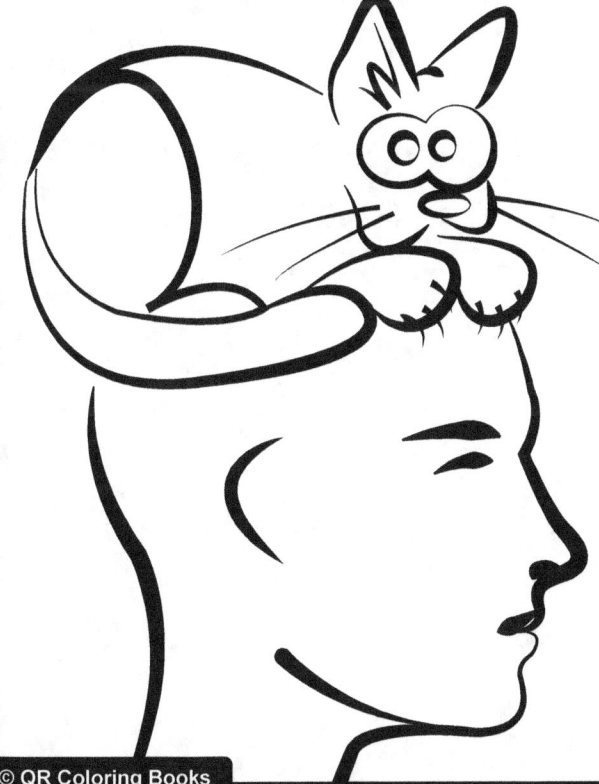

Cat Nip

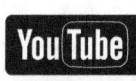

CAT FIGHT

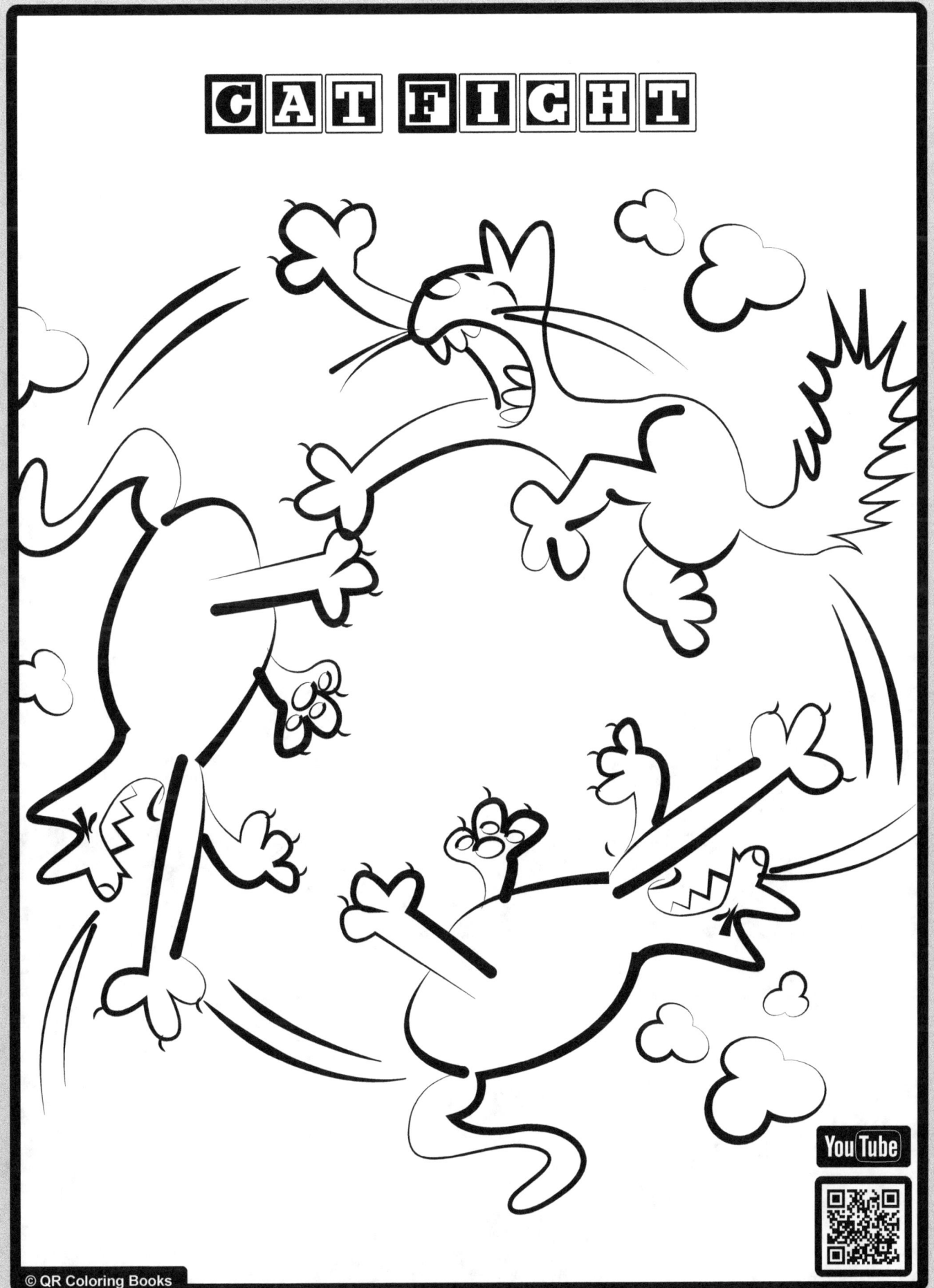

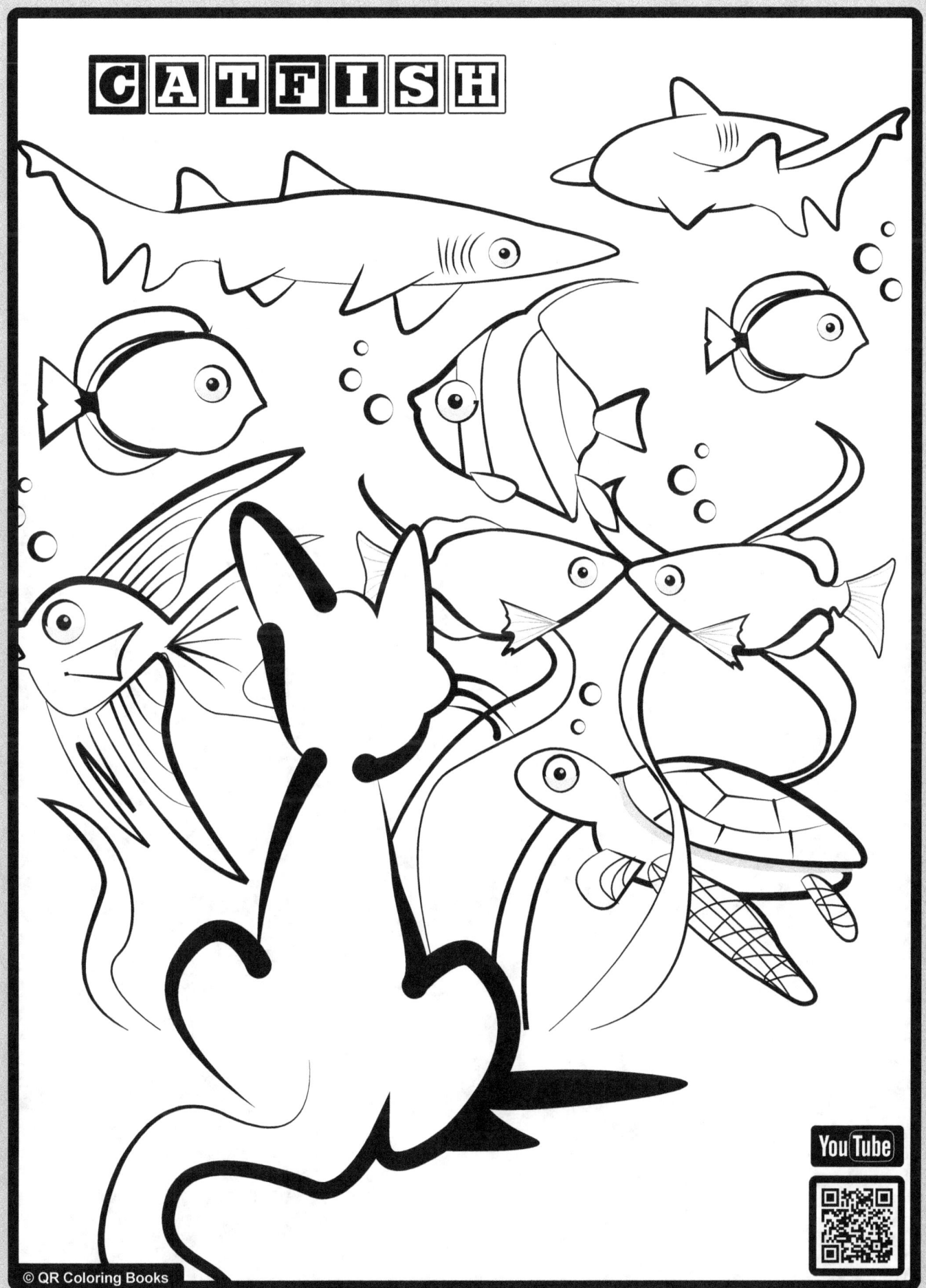

CATFISH

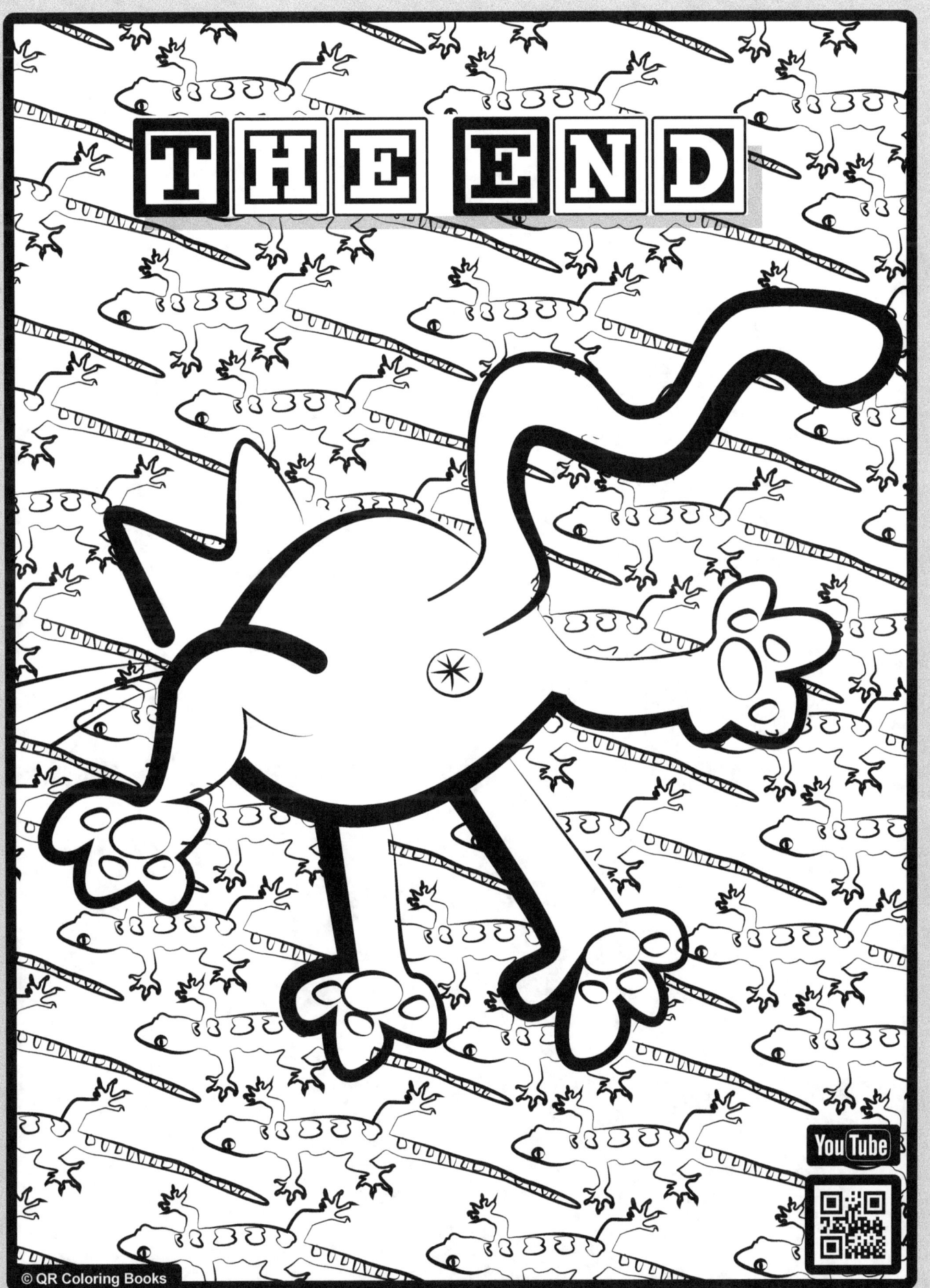

THE END

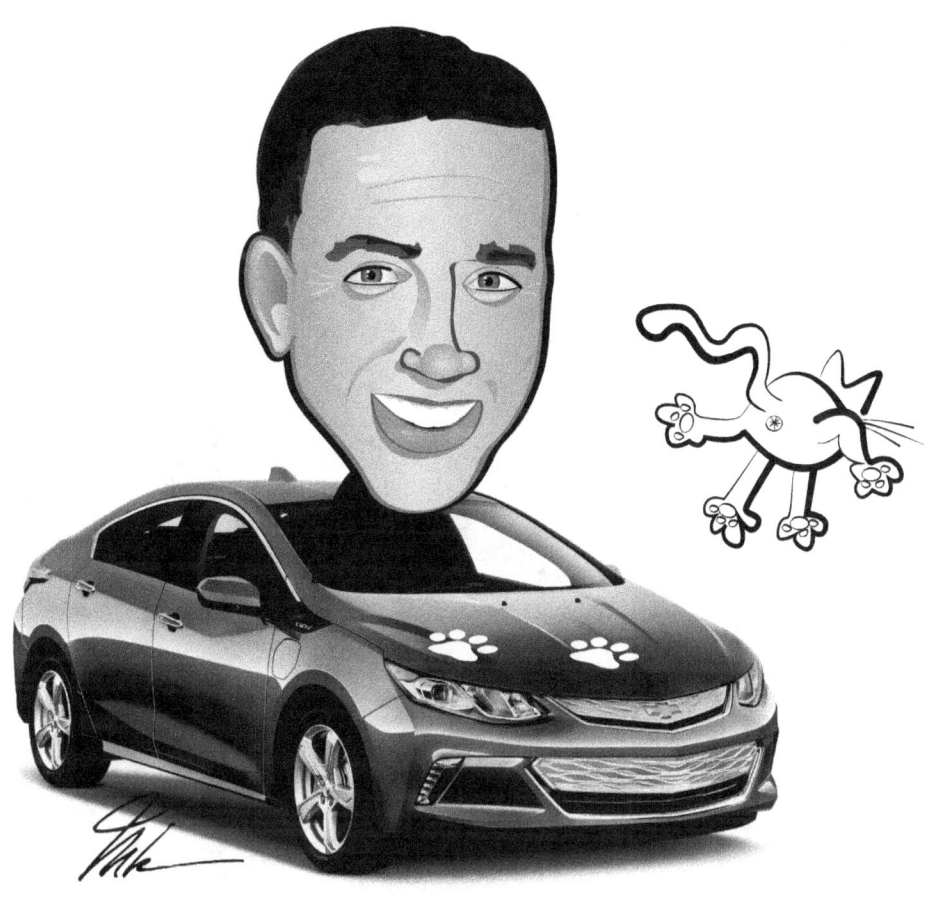

Created by:
Mike Browne

The Crazy Cat Coloring Book was created from cartoons
I drew of my cat Bailey. He was my best pal for
15 years. He would sit on my lap for hours while I draw.

QR Coloring Books are a little different in that they
incorporate both tactile drawing and YouTube videos.

Turn on some music, grab a crayon, your cellphone
and kick back in your favorite chair.

Have fun coloring!